THE ACCIDENTAL ALPHA WOMAN

THE GUIDE TO THRIVING WHEN LIFE FEELS OVERWHELMING

KAREN WRIGHT

Difference Press

McLean, Virginia, USA

Published 2020

Cover Design: Jennifer Stimson

Author Photo: Eric Michael Pearson

CONTENTS

For Dave.

"The road is long and the world is small."

And yes, you were right.

1

WHY ARE YOU HERE?

You are a woman. You are tough. Capable. Strong.

You can do it all.

You are a masterful juggler and a stoic manager. You keep families and businesses functioning, communities organized, and events running like clockwork.

For many of you, the busy life you live is what you chose, and while it's not perfect, well, what is?

For the rest of you, though, your lot in life has ended up being quite different than what you'd envisioned for yourself, and if you are perfectly honest, it kind of sucks. At the very least, it's harder than you expected, and you are shouldering a much heavier load than you had anticipated. You're kind of lonely and pretty tired, and you aren't even sure who you are or what you want anymore, but since you have responsibilities and people relying on you, you keep soldiering on.

Whether or not you think you can handle the challenges, obligations, and occasionally difficult circumstances that have come your way, you do handle them, don't you? Because what choice do you have? In fact, in many cases, the unexpected challenges just motivate you to hunker down and power through and be fiercely independent, or at least so focused you don't look beyond what you are handling.

But what if that precise tendency to "handle" everything – the relentless juggling act that includes everyone and everything except YOU – ends up being the biggest barrier between you and a life of ease and happiness?

What if your reluctance to be vulnerable and messy, to be different than what "people" expect, to maybe admit that you are scared and tired and overwhelmed, and to ask for help is the reason you feel isolated and exhausted?

What if putting your needs and interests on the back burner indefinitely costs you your identity and erodes your sense of self?

What if "strong" is your biggest impediment to real contentment and happiness?

I've felt grief, anger, frustration, and shame at being in a situation that was not what it was "supposed to be," at not seeing what others apparently saw clearly, and at being in a mess that I "should have" known better than to find myself in.

The disconnect is the problem, or the root of it, anyway – the "this is not what I signed up for" problem. The difference between what you think life is "supposed to" look like (happy, healthy, fun, connected) and what it ends up being is that point of tension that creates an issue. The disconnect is what you resist, and it's the reason why you throw yourself into coping mode. After all, "doing" is oddly easier than facing reality and admitting vulnerability. And, at least in my experience, it's the precursor to the bigger problem.

You became this island of stoicism and of coping and handling. You figure that asking for help would be embarrassing, time-consuming, expensive, or complicated, or would show "people" that you're weak. Or, worse, incapable. But as the disconnect becomes clearer and the load gets heavier, the circle of support gets smaller because you don't let people in.

And on top of all of that, when you are overwhelmed, tired, and struggling with your numerous roles and demands, it's hard to be around people who seem to have it easier.

It doesn't matter how you got here. You might be finding your joy and success in a climb up the corporate ladder only to find that you're still expected to handle all of the major responsibilities on the home front. You might have started a business that's growing, and while it's having an impact and generating good money, it's demanding more of your time and energy, and you're feeling like the single point of failure both at home and at work. You might be suddenly partner-less – whether by divorce or illness or other unanticipated circumstance – and you're doing it all by yourself. Or you might have envisioned a life with a partner, but so far, you're doing life solo, and sometimes being alone feels, well, lonely. Whatever your particular and unique set of circumstances, chances are that you handle responsibilities and care for so many and yet the one you actively care for the least is usually yourself.

Being strong is lonely.

What's the solution?

Based on the combination of personal experience (and lessons hard-learned) and what I know and practice as an executive coach, in this book, I offer you a framework and some ideas that will help you look at your life clearly, make conscious, self-aware choices about your path and build some support mechanisms around you that will help you sustain your changes.

I'm going to help you get better at being able to RECEIVE.

Getting better at receiving starts with a mindset shift. Receiving is not a weakness. In fact, by the time you're done here, I want you to appreciate the ability to receive as being a sign of the kind of strength that is truly, uniquely female.

At your core, you are a collaborator and a relationship builder. You are intuitive and compassionate. You are nurturing and fierce. You just need to get better at doing and being those things for yourself and understanding that doing *for* yourself does not mean doing it *all* yourself.

As I share the tools and ideas that I think can help you, I'll share part of my story and those of a few of my clients and friends. You'll meet some women who were confronted with enormous challenges and who figured it out, some who've made a few small tweaks that have resulted in them feeling better about themselves, and some who are still on the path but headed in the right direction.

I hope you'll see a bit of yourself in some of these stories and that you'll try at least a few of the things I suggest here. But I warn you, it will mean you'll have to put yourself first (at least some of the time) and ask for some help. Get ready to RECEIVE.

2

MY STORY

We were in the kitchen, preparing dinner for our two boys who, at the time, were aged four and six years old. I was in the early years of my coaching practice, while Mr. X (my now former husband), the brilliant marketing entrepreneur, had been having some struggles with his business as he tried to take it in a new direction. We had been sharing household expenses since we'd moved in together ten years prior, which worked reasonably well most of the time. As we made the meal, we chatted, mostly about the small events of our day. Then...

"I won't be able to put money in the mortgage account this week," he said.

I asked him what he meant.

"I don't have money to put in the mortgage account."

"How is that possible? What's going on?" I started to feel the panic rising.

"I haven't landed any clients with the new line of business, and I've exhausted all my backup funds paying the staff and covering the office rent. I don't have any personal money available at the moment."

"What do you mean you've 'exhausted all your back up funds?' You mean contingency funds in the business, right, so you can't take a salary?"

He shifted uncomfortably. "Well, not exactly. I've been covering the business shortfall for a while."

"Meaning?"

"My credit cards are over their limits, and I've withdrawn from my retirement account."

"How much?" I stammered.

Turns out, the answer was "all of it." He not only had nothing; he was in the hole. We were in the hole. And he didn't tell me.

Rather than be transparent with me – or probably even himself – about the state of his business, Mr. X had done massive damage to our financial situation without apparent regard for the fact that we had a mortgage and two kids in private school. I'd already been struggling to keep up with my half of the expenses, what with the demands of early-stage motherhood and a still-developing business. I was instantly overwhelmed with multiple emotions: terror at the financial crisis in front of me, panic at the immediate need to figure out what had to be done to keep us afloat, and betrayal at the hands of the person I thought I could trust most in the world, who had apparently been keeping massive secrets.

I come from a long line of independent (to a fault, as it turns out), problem-solving, pragmatic women. Give me a hurdle, and I'll clear it, and I'll make sure that everyone along the way has fresh muffins and is on time for their activities, all the while staying firmly in denial about the reality of my situation.

But an instantaneous change in everything I believed about the fundamentals of my marriage and my life?

What came next provides the foundation for this book.

However, this isn't just another story of a woman's struggle and eventual arrival at herself.

What makes my story unique is that, professionally, I'm in the business of self-awareness. Of life planning. Of overcoming obstacles. Of goal achievement. Of reading people. Of clear and effective communication. Of devising strategies based on an objective view of reality. I'm a master-level certified professional executive coach. I know how human behaviour, motivation, self-reflection, choices, and accountability work.

But, as my good friend Charlie says, "You can't read the label from inside the jar."

Or, as I like to think of it, "My hindsight is better than most."

As I look back on where I was – in the kitchen on that pivotal day and, if I'm honest, for a few years before that – I wish I'd known and used some of the things that over time have become daily staples in my client work. I wish I'd recognized that my beliefs about being "strong" were building a massive barrier to my ability to see what was going on, take control of my life, ask for and accept help, and be the gracious recipient of intuitive messages and opportunities to reflect and grow.

My goal here is to save you the time and trouble of my more than two hundred hours of coach training, certifications in positive psychology and health coaching, some study in neuroscience, and a license to train mindfulness. I'm bringing all that plus the stories and wisdom gained from tens of thousands of hours spent in deep, intimate, privileged conversation with smart people who were getting in their own way just like I did.

I'm going to share my story and tell you what I'd do if I had a do-over – if I'd known then what I know now. And I'm going to give you a peek behind the curtain at the ways I've worked with women over my two decades as a coach with examples of the exercises and processes I've used to help them shift – first their mindsets, and then their lives.

Hopefully, if you see yourself at any of the stages

of my story or the stories from the other women, you can use the tools and frameworks I offer here to accelerate your journey through whatever is going sideways in your life, to get you more quickly toward a life of more ease, more support, more asking for what you need, and more comfort in receiving.

3

THE RECEIVE FRAMEWORK

My experience, both personal and with clients, tells me that many women – at least those who characterize themselves as "strong" by necessity – are usually pretty terrible at one thing in particular: receiving.

I'm talking about the act of allowing input, assistance, ideas, moral support, tokens of appreciation, compliments, intuitive messages, and gifts of magical serendipity from the universe – all of it. Accepting kindness and offerings of time and attention. Accepting reality and receiving the opportunities inherent in changed circumstances. Taking what you need when you need it even if – and especially if – someone else needs something.

Under normal circumstances, you probably create your life in a reasonably sustainable way. But throw a curveball, a surprise, an event, a major incident, or a shift in conditions your way, and receiving might just make the difference between barely surviving and thriving.

Shortly after I separated from my kids' dad, I signed up for an entrepreneurial immersion program with the brilliant Jonathan Fields where fifteen of us, all business owners, gathered several times over the course of a year to work on creating our businesses as enterprises that would support each of us living our "good life." At each live event, we took turns sharing our progress and our challenges.

One participant, a creative, determined young woman trying to make a big shift in her business, used her time at one event to share all of her ideas and the frenetic level of activity she had undertaken since our last meeting. While she was sharing, numerous of the rest of us were piping up with suggestions and offers – connections, resources, creative ideas, and direct assistance. She barely acknowledged the offers and instead described the great long list of things she intended to do before our next event. Finally, in exasperated frustration, one of the program leaders burst out, "You SUCK at receiving."

She was so convinced that she had to do it all that she completely missed the gifts that were coming at her in an avalanche of kindness and expertise. As a result, she was well along the path to guaranteeing that achieving what she wanted to achieve would be done in the most difficult way possible – alone.

I've seen this pattern over and over again, and I believe it's the biggest barrier to true happiness as a strong, purpose-driven, and, dare I say, alpha woman. Because these days, aren't we all – at least to some degree – alpha women?

I'm sure that some of you are resisting that idea, so before I go any further, let me unpack it a bit.

An alpha woman is strong, confident, and a leader – not necessarily by role or title, but certainly by demeanour. An alpha woman handles a lot, makes decisions easily, and makes things happen. Not all women choose to show up as an alpha, but we all have it in us because we are the problem-solvers, the figure-it-out-ers, and the do-what-needs-to-be-done-ers.

All that said, I believe that there are two different types of alpha women: accidental and intentional. On the surface, they seem similar – the behaviours, the drive, and the ability to juggle are all common to both types. What's different is how they feel, and that's often a function of how they ended up in the alpha role. What's usually also true is that the size and weight of the load they carry is different, because only one of the types usually knows what is hers to carry and what can and should be dumped, delegated, or at least deferred.

An Intentional Alpha is a woman who

consciously chooses to be the leader in her life. Her various life roles are all designed to give her the freedom to be who she is and to do what she does. The Intentional Alpha is unapologetically strong and yet doesn't attempt to be all things to all people. She knows who she is and what she does well, and the people she includes in her life love that about her. She delegates comfortably, feeling no shame or guilt in saying no. She's comfortable in her skin. She's forceful, capable, and responsible, and she likes it that way. If she has a partner, the relationship has been negotiated to ensure she's got the room to soar. If she doesn't have a partner, it may be by choice, or at the least, not having one is not interfering with her ability to lead her best life.

The Accidental Alpha, on the other hand, ended up in the alpha role by – you guessed it – accident. This woman never intended to be shouldering the entire load for her life and isn't happy about the fact that it's turned out that way. The pathways into life as an Accidental Alpha are varied and include things like divorce, spousal job loss, or illness, never having found a life partner, or any number of other complexes, unexpected circumstances, and responsibilities. The common thread is the disconnect with what she envisioned and the resistance to or lack of acceptance of her true reality. Being stuck in resistance creates barriers to everything that can make life easier and happier.

While I believe that there are ideas here that can be useful to both types of alpha women, this book is directly targeted to the Accidental Alpha because – like the kitchen story in the previous chapter hints – it's where I found myself. One of my goals for this book is to take you Accidental Alphas on a journey toward being more Intentional.

Life isn't linear, and neither should any framework that purports to help you survive it be.

That said, I crafted this journey based on my story and my progression from one stage to the next and fine-tuned it through work with clients over the years, and if you're in the early stages of figuring something out, you might start at the beginning and follow along sequentially. Here's a brief overview of the framework I offer: RECEIVE:

R: Recognize Your Reality. I begin with Recognizing Your Reality because you can't solve something without being clear about what the problem is. The path toward your solution begins at the point where you have a crystal-clear understanding of your current situation, and oddly this is frequently the most difficult thing to accomplish.

E: Evaluate. Next is Evaluating, because any given situation will mean different things to different people, and the same situation can mean something different at a different moment in time. Understanding the role that your values and timing play in how you feel about something gives you a better chance of finding a way forward that feels better than where you are.

C: Choose. Once you know what your situation means to you, you can Choose – set yourself on a course that makes sense given what's important. Because we truly do have choices – the biggest problem is often that none of the obvious choices seem acceptable or appealing, not to mention the idea of cutting off a path of action or deciding against something is counter to our "have it all" culture. You may need to go against the flow of the world to move forward, but you can do it with conviction if you've done the groundwork to prepare yourself.

E: Energy. From there, you learn to manage your energy. You can do it all, just not all at once, and meting out your energy ensures you move consistently toward what's important, rather than what's easiest or most conveniently in front of you. Your energy requires constant attention because it's in constant flux. Learn how to pay attention to it and ensure you've consistently got what you need available when you need it.

I: Initiate. Wouldn't it be wonderful if the people around you just "knew" what you needed when you need it? Sadly, that's rarely the case. Rather than suffer – or worse, wallow – learn that you have to Initiate to get what you need, and there are ways to ask that won't feel icky.

V: Voice. The clearer you are about who you are

and what's important to you, the more life tends to feel easier and happier. Yet in the midst of "adulting," you may have lost track of what lights you up. Here's where you will find and express your unique Voice.

E: Ease. Yes, life can be easier. Once you've put yourself on the path that's best and most right for you, it's possible to create a life that has a little more Ease. To help you sustain yourself as you move forward, you'll learn about simple ways to stay connected to what's important.

There you have it. R-E-C-E-I-V-E.

To illustrate the framework, I share my own stories and experiences as well as examples of how I've used these principles both personally and with clients, along with some reflections based on what I might have done differently if I'd had the benefit of my professional experience when I was in the midst of my journey. I've also featured a number of client stories – used either anonymously or with permission – that I think reflect the multitude of circumstances that might be the entry points into being an Accidental Alpha.

I offer this all in hopes that it helps you learn to RECEIVE.

4

R – RECOGNIZE YOUR REALITY. WHAT'S GOING ON?

In coaching, we talk about the "gap" – the distance between where you currently are and where you want to be. That distance is where you work so that you can make progress toward that desired endpoint. But in order to do the right work, you have to have a clear sense of the real starting point.

Or, put another way, you have to recognize and accept the current reality.

To accept reality is often to accept some level of discomfort because it means you've been choosing to see things differently than they are in order to cope. And I don't know about you, but I'm positively masterful at overlooking something I don't want to see. But it's impossible to come up with a decent plan if you're building it on quicksand.

When life goes sideways – or the minute you

realize that life has gone sideways – the first step is accepting that something is seriously unacceptable. It's not a tiny, little aberration; it's not a teeny, little bump in the road or a temporary blip. It's an absolute recognition of, "This is major, this is different, this is not what I planned, what I wanted, or what I thought I'd ever have to handle."

Once you're there, you can deal.

Anything you do to strategize before accepting whatever your new reality is will be a flawed plan because it's not based on truth.

The sooner you accept the reality of whatever is going on, the sooner you'll be able to process the completely normal but not terribly useful anger you likely feel because you're in a situation you didn't expect or sign up for.

TIME PASSED

Sometime after the kitchen conversation – and by "sometime" I mean more than five years – I found myself in a midday message exchange with my husband. He'd had a few business ideas since shutting down his original company, none of which had gone anywhere. I was trying to be patient, supportive, and loyal, and on this particular day, the conversation related to a dream project he wanted to pursue. The best possible timeline on this dream project, he informed me, was about two years.

Two. More. Years.

Two more years of me earning the money and handling most of what went on at home and with our boys.

Two more years of me feeling like the walls were closing in.

Two more years of not getting any kind of real support from my partner.

You get the idea.

In that moment, something clicked. In that moment, it was clear to me that I had spent the previous five or more years telling myself a story that, as time went on, had less and less chance of being true.

I had painted a largely imaginary (and certainly idealistic) picture of me as the long-suffering, ever-patient, steadfastly loyal, and loving partner to a creative, entrepreneurial genius who was just going through a "rough patch," struggling to find his next big opportunity. It was just a matter of time, and then everything would be fine.

But really, we were in a dysfunctional stalemate where I was increasingly resentful that he wasn't stepping up either financially or in the caregiver role, while he repeatedly conceived of and abandoned new "big ideas." While I wanted to be the kind of person who could accept him for who and what he was or wasn't, the truth was that I was in a situation that was unacceptable, not to mention a relationship that was operating on a different set of principles than I'd signed up for. I was angry, broke, tired, and lonely most of the time.

It's natural to avoid that which causes pain or, worse, that which rocks the foundation upon which you've built your life. Ignoring the truth, minimizing the issues, and covering dysfunction with activity and responsibility is a strategy that can work until, suddenly, it no longer does.

JEN

My client, Jen, was an outgoing, accomplished, intelligent woman – single, in her mid-forties, and living well by any standard. She worked hard, to be sure, but every chance she got, she travelled. From ski vacations and golf junkets to tennis lessons in exotic locations, she was out there. When she wasn't away somewhere exciting, she enjoyed theatre, sports, activities at a couple of local private clubs, and lots of great dinners out with friends.

Then one day, she arrived at a coaching session with an announcement.

"I've had a profound epiphany."

She went on, "I just turned forty-five, and I've just realized that I'm living my life as if someone is eventually going to take care of me, as if the man of my dreams will soon arrive and we'll sail happily off into the sunset together."

I was confused. "Well, what's wrong with that? Doesn't everyone hope for that, at least on some level?"

She explained, "I'm not talking about wanting romance. I'm talking about the fact that I've been spending and living with total disregard for my long-term financial well-being. I've been living as if, at some point soon, someone would come along and take me under their wing and at least share if not provide for me. I've been waiting without planning for the possibility that my white knight might not appear. And, at my age, I've just realized that there's an increasing chance that he might not ever show up. All of a sudden, I'm feeling scared – like I've been financially reckless and irresponsible."

Jen had just confronted herself with a different version of reality than she'd been perceiving for most of her life. Once she'd seen her situation, she was in a position to take steps that aligned with that new view of reality.

From that new point of recognition, Jen and I were able to have different coaching conversations. We worked to unpack the various choices she had made in the past that were at odds with her new, clearer view of her reality. Jen became clear on where she'd been hoping and dreaming and where she'd been turning a blind eye to what was happening. Over the course of a few sessions, Jen was able to create a helpful distinction between her feelings and assumptions and the facts she most needed in order to plan for her future in a realistic way. Jen ended up with a financial plan, a real estate investment, and a list of the travel adventures she wanted to have, as well as a commitment to resist impulses and temptations if they ran counter to her savings and investment goals. She's still doing the fun things, but she's now doing them with the knowledge that she's also taking care of her future.

HOW TO RECOGNIZE YOUR REALITY

Removing your filters and your rose-coloured glasses is hard; after all, it's impossible to be objective when you're a central character in a situation or, as we say in coaching, when you are "attached to the outcome." That said, there are some things you can try in order to push some of your impeding perceptions aside.

- What are you telling yourself about your current situation or your life? Write it down. All of it. Write down everything you believe, feel, experience, and assume about whatever you're struggling with. Dig deep here.
- Now take a separate page and divide it into two columns.
- Take a look at what you wrote above and

start to dissect it. Extract the immutable facts, the observable data, and the crystal-clear characteristics and descriptions of what's going on. Put all of that in the left column.

- Down the other side, list the stories, feelings, perceptions, and assumptions that you've woven into your version of what's going on.
- Now look at your lists and double-check their accuracy by asking these questions of every item: Is this a fact or a story? Is this a fact or a belief? Is this a fact or an assumption? Is this a fact or a feeling? Check yourself often here – if you've been in denial for a while, some of your stories are going to feel like they are facts.

Take a look at the two columns. If you've sorted things appropriately, you will probably feel emotion when you read the right column and a more calm, clinical frame of mind when you're looking at the left side.

Once you've got a list of facts, you've got the foundation upon which to take the next step.

IF I'D KNOWN THEN WHAT I KNOW NOW

My younger self suffered a massive need to be liked, especially by men. I've done enough therapy to know that having a distant father with a bad temper is one of the root causes of that need.

That younger self was terrified of making a man angry.

And terrified that a man might leave.

I didn't see any relationship between what I was willing to endure in order to keep the peace and my sense of self-worth.

When I found myself confronted with unavoidable facts in that kitchen conversation and for quite a while afterward, I went immediately to old patterns – hope, peacekeeping, helpfulness, avoidance, compliance, and even co-creation. I stayed with the story that felt comforting to me and that I thought would please others rather than confront something that was scary and full of risk and uncertainty.

What I know now is that the longer you stay in denial of the facts, the longer and more difficult it is before you can accurately assess a situation and move forward toward your solution.

SHE FIGURED IT OUT

When I met Sarah, she and her husband had been married for about twenty years. Over that period of time, Robert had started about a dozen businesses and had undertaken several other professional pursuits. Some took off, some didn't.

Sarah is a serious, hard-working, financially conservative, organized person. Bills get paid on time, money gets put away for a rainy day, and the kids have college funds.

They met in university, and Sarah says she was always drawn to Robert's sense of wonder and possibility. "He has an idea a minute and more when he meets new people, which is all the time because he'll talk to anyone anywhere."

When they decided to get married, Sarah had no illusions about who'd need to be the "responsible" one.

Sarah has worked for the same company since she graduated from college, and while she enjoys what she does, she also understands that her stability gives Robert room to dream.

Sarah knows exactly who Robert is and knows that he lightens her up. Robert is a loving husband, a great dad, an active contributor to and participant in the local community, and a fantastic cook, so for Sarah, it's an easy trade-off.

Sarah made a choice to be the breadwinner and to handle the financial responsibilities of their lives because she feels supported in other ways that are important to her. She has had her moments of doubt and frustration, but any time she's felt that way, we've worked together to reconnect her with her initial choices and the current facts of her situation to determine whether anything fundamental has changed. So far, the facts that guided her into a marriage and life where she provides the financial stability in exchange for numerous other valuable forms of support haven't changed, so she understands her occasional moments of frustration to be just that – moments.

Sarah clearly sees her reality and is happy.

REFLECTION

The "strong" woman would rather buckle down, take action, and solve problems than reflect, get uncomfortable, and be uncertain about what comes next. The "strong" woman will power fiercely onward, reluctant to admit weakness or failure or to bother anyone else with her struggles. For those of you who've gotten used to handling whatever comes your way, you usually prefer not to spend much time reflecting on what it all means.

If I wanted to add a quote here, there are many to choose from. Gandhi reportedly said that the journey of a thousand miles begins with a single step. Twelve-step recovery programs tell us that in order to find a solution, we first must admit we have a problem. Johnny Nash musically informed us that we can see clearly once the rain is gone.

The point is that you can't see where you want to go unless you know exactly where you are starting. The first step in recreating your life as one where you can thrive and feel fully supported is the step that ensures you examine the truth of what's happening for real.

Only with that clarity about your reality can you figure out what it all means.

5

E – EVALUATE YOUR EXPERIENCE

We all have filters – lenses through which we see and process the world. A surprising number of those filters are developed at a young age, courtesy of our childhood experiences, and usually at the hands of our family members.

What that means is that your interpretation of any experience or situation will be uniquely yours. Not your best friend's, not your colleague's, not your neighbour's – yours.

Because your interpretation is uniquely yours, it's not right or wrong. You feel how you feel, you believe what you believe, and you value what you value. When something changes, it might mean other things need to change, and only you can know that for yourself.

The other thing to consider is your timeline.

There are probably a lot of difficult situations you can handle if they are true for a short period of time. Extend that timeline, though, and you may feel differently.

On top of all of that, you have to also be able to monitor yourself and tell yourself the truth. What might be considered a noble stance to take for a while might eventually become a crutch and a reason to avoid a difficult reality. I'm looking at you over-nurturers out there.

The conversation about the dream project was a pivotal moment for me. The minute I knew I was finally seeing things clearly, I realized I had to figure out what was next. Continuing in miserable ignorance was no longer an option once the real situation was evident and once I'd taken the blinders off and was confronting the facts. I needed a plan.

A bit of background might be helpful here. I grew up in a situation where my mother was completely reliant on my father for money. That wasn't unusual back then, and it wouldn't have been a problem except that my father was a retailer, and while he was charming and great with the customers, he wasn't the best businessperson. That meant that some weeks, he didn't have any money to bring home, leaving my mother unable to buy groceries.

I don't recall ever having a Scarlett O'Hara moment, swearing that I'd never let that happen to me, but I do know that safety when it comes to money is something I value highly. When choosing a life partner, I tried hard to ensure that I was teaming up with someone who would be responsible, who I could trust to make good financial decisions, and who valued financial stability.

When I met Mr. X, he was a well-educated, intelligent, driven, and successful entrepreneur from a wealthy family. I was educated, hard-working, and successful in my own right. We ventured into a life together as equals – shared vision, shared financial responsibilities – all balanced and logical.

So little wonder why I was taken aback when he made the kitchen announcement. But I'd made a commitment, and I have always been reluctant to admit that I'm wrong. In that initial moment, I made a quick assessment.

I told him, "Shut your company down. Stop the bleeding. I'll get a job."

I had a standing offer for an executive-level job with a former boss, and it was time to accept his offer for the sake of my family. I didn't analyze the situation in depth; I just leapt to what I thought was a short-term solution.

I didn't wonder how long we'd be in this situation or consider the impact it might have on our relationship. I just knew that there was a problem to be solved right away, so I solved it. At the time, I had no reason to believe this was going to be my "new normal."

But scroll ahead, and it had been five years of me shouldering, well, too much. And once I realized that we were likely to be in the status quo for at least two more years, my evaluation was quite different than it had been back in the kitchen. I realized that being expected to carry all of the financial responsibility meant something different after five years than it did when it seemed to be a heroic gesture to solve a short-term problem.

TRISH

Trish worked for a particularly difficult person. Her boss was legendary in his manipulative behaviour, his womanizing, his self-centredness, his alcohol abuse – the list went on. But he was running an organization that did good work – work for which Trish had a lot of heart and to which she'd been committed for many years. Still, though, I often wondered how she did it, how she kept on working for this guy. I asked her, and she said, "I love the work that I get to do, and as long as I know I'm making an impact, I can tolerate a lot. But you're right; he's not easy to work for, and for a long time, I found myself bouncing back and forth almost daily, asking myself whether the value I place on the work was enough to offset the way he behaves with not just me but the rest of the team. And while I know I have choices, asking myself the question every day was stressful. I devised a new approach.

"On the first day of every month, I look at myself in the mirror and ask myself whether, for the next month, I can be all in. If the answer is yes, I don't ask myself the question again until the first of the next month, so I take the question out of my consciousness and am better able to focus on the work. And if there comes a time when my answer to myself is no, that I don't think I can do it for another month, well then that will be my time to leave."

Trish saw the situation for what it was and recognized that there might come a time when she would no longer be able to tolerate all that went on. She knew she had to evaluate whether she could stay there on a regular basis, but she also knew that being "in the question" every day would be exhausting. She established a time frame that worked for her so she knew exactly how long she would be committed to continuing and how often she would be able to re-examine her choice. And she gave herself permission to make a different choice if and when she no longer felt that the work was worth what it took to work with the difficult boss.

HOW TO EVALUATE YOUR EXPERIENCE

You've got your list of the facts and the stories you've been telling yourself about the facts.

Now it's time to dig a little deeper.

- Think back to times in your life when you've been in a situation that's been wonderful in every way. You've loved the people, the activities, the environment – everything about whatever it was. See if you can come up with a few examples like this, maybe three or four.
- Now think of times in your life when you've felt the opposite. Think of times when you've felt outraged, conflicted, or helpless. Again, see if you can come up with three or four of those.
- When you look at the first group, see if you can notice any common themes or characteristics. Did they all involve creativity, service, or overcoming an obstacle? Once you figure out what these positive or "flow" experiences have in common, you'll have identified some of your core values.
- When you look at the second group and do the same thing, the common theme or characteristics are likely situations where your values have most likely been compromised or violated.
- Now, you've got a list of the things that are important to you, either as guiding

principles for your life or as non-negotiable boundaries.

- Next, look back at the facts of your situation as you listed them in the last chapter. Do the immutable characteristics of your situation support and align with your values, or are they at odds? If you've got disconnects or misalignments, you are probably looking at a situation that's going to require some decisions.
- While you're doing this, please take the time to notice when you are resisting identifying a value. For example, whether I like it or not, whether or not it feels mature or admirable, I place a high value on what to others are probably small, inconsequential signs of respect (which for me includes things like manners and punctuality). I've found that I cannot stay in any kind of relationship – friend, client, or partner – with someone who doesn't demonstrate what to me are non-negotiable signs of respect. It's my job to be clear with myself and with other people what's important to me in this category. And if the others choose not to demonstrate respect the way I value it, I'm in a position to make an informed choice

about whether I want to continue that relationship.

More than twenty years of working with coaching clients has shown me over and over again that if there is a mismatch at a values level, it's difficult to reconcile.

IF I'D KNOWN THEN WHAT I KNOW NOW

When I was younger, I'd bend over backward to accommodate, to be liked, and to not upset or disrupt.

I never got good at saying what worked for me or what made me happy or unhappy.

My early relationships were filled with violations of boundaries I didn't even realize I could have.

My today self realizes that while our early wiring can be pretty hard to dismantle, it's something we always need to be working on.

My younger self might have let that untenable situation continue for longer.

My today self wouldn't have allowed it to continue for as long as it did.

ME

As soon as we finished the message exchange about the dream project, I called my lawyer. I explained the situation and that I needed to consider some pretty drastic options.

Ever practical, my lawyer asked, “But doesn’t he come from money?”

I said yes, that he did come from family money, but that he wasn’t willing to ask his mother for help.

“How old is his mother?”

“In her eighties,” I responded.

“Can you wait her out?”

While on some level that seemed funny, it wasn’t the craziest idea in the world. Wait out the mother-in-law, so Mr. X would inherit her fortune and all would be solved.

Except the mother-in-law comes from a family where people live into their hundreds. And in her eighties, she was still driving and playing tennis.

But thinking that idea through, notwithstanding it being crass and ridiculous, was useful. Could I hang in for another five or ten years? Nope, that plan or any other that would require me to live with the status quo for much longer was way beyond my ability to tolerate what was going on, given I’d already decided that the situation as it stood after five years was no longer something I could live with.

I knew, with certainty I’d not felt before, that I couldn’t wait anymore. I couldn’t keep on hoping and being loyal and having faith that everything would work out.

My evaluation told me I had to do something.

SHE FIGURED IT OUT

My client Ellen's husband had been diagnosed with a rare, incurable, slowly debilitative brain disease.

She cared for him and watched him deteriorate for ten years.

I'd always liked and had great respect for this smart, talented, vivacious woman. Ellen makes things happen. To watch her deal with this was hard – although nothing like it must have been for her to handle.

And over the time we had worked together, Ellen had wrestled with what felt like conflicting values: her loyalty and marital commitment versus her acceptance of the inevitable outcome of this devastating situation.

Then one day, a year or so after she'd made the choice to move her husband into long-term care, we got together for lunch. One of the first things I noticed was that Ellen wasn't wearing her wedding ring.

"I love him, and I mean no disrespect. But this situation has been going on for many years, and there is only one possible outcome. And while I continue to be loyal and will continue to visit him and be responsible for his care, it's time for me to accept that my life will need to go forward without him."

Ellen had figured out how to honour her values

of respect and loyalty while accepting the reality of her situation and understanding that, with an eye toward the path forward, she had to own her choices in a way that ensured she was taking care of herself. Resisting the reality of her husband's illness served Ellen well for a period of time – until one day, it didn't. Accepting what the illness meant and what impact it would have on her life allowed Ellen to move forward and to take concrete action that was more likely to help her be happy than keep her stuck in a mental version of life that just was no longer true and would never be.

REFLECTION

For those of you who tend to be nurturing, it's difficult to let go of hope. Add loyalty, pride, and whatever you think "other people" will say about you into the mix, and course-correcting on the basis of your interests feels pretty uncomfortable.

You nurture bad situations, bad jobs, and bad relationships. Hell, I've known women who live with bad haircuts to avoid switching stylists or having a tough conversation.

But when you confront yourself with an unequivocally values-based issue, you've crossed into territory where doing nothing is the thing that becomes untenable.

By confronting what you're most conflicted or

upset about, you put yourself in a position to ascertain what you need more of or what you have to let go of. Rarely are any of these evaluations easy, and more often than not, they require that you dig deep and overcome some resistance to something you've been avoiding, but not doing the evaluation step means you're not equipped for what comes next.

Your next step is to figure out what your choices are. And make no mistake, you have choices. You just might not like some of them.

6

C – CHOOSE YOUR COURSE, AND COMMIT TO IT

One of our biggest problems is that we have too many choices because we truly have virtually unlimited options as to how we can live our lives these days. I find that most of my clients get stuck in one of two buckets: saying yes to everything, which leads to confusion, diluted effort, and no real commitment to any one path forward, or not choosing at all, which, make no mistake, is a choice in and of itself. They are often stuck in either overwhelm or inertia.

My good friend Charlie Gilkey, productivity expert and author of the fantastic book, "Start Finishing," is adamant that humans can only take on so many things at once.

Feeling overwhelmed? Charlie will probably say you've taken on "too many projects."

And just to be clear, Charlie defines anything that

occupies a significant portion of your time, effort, and attention as a project. So, are you moving from one home to another? That's a project. Are you a primary caregiver to children? A project. Job? A project. Competitive sport participation? A project. First-on-call to an invalid relative? A project. New creative undertaking? A project. Tactical and logistics support for kids with several activities? A project (and maybe more than one). You get the idea. And, at least according to Charlie, the appropriate number of projects most people ought to attempt at one time is between three and five, depending on the scope, scale, complexity, and duration.

Too often, both in my personal experience and in the lives of clients I've worked with over the years, the reluctance to confront a tough situation and to make a difficult choice results in saying yes to too many easy things as camouflage for confronting the hard things and changing or eliminating some and eventually leads up to an overloading of responsibilities, roles, and, yes, projects.

Or – and I see this less often – you choose nothing at all (which, remember, is a choice), leaving you unable to move in any direction.

Why is choosing – or deciding – so difficult? Why do people put it off for so long?

Enter #FOMO – fear of missing out – and its cousin, analysis paralysis.

Choosing is definitive. Making an unequivocal

choice means, by definition, that you are eliminating all other options. And that feels scary because what if you choose the wrong path? I see people either choosing everything to make sure they don't miss anything or eliminate something great or getting paralyzed in trying to choose the perfect thing and ultimately choose nothing.

But here's the thing: no matter what you choose, you'll never know for sure how the other option would have turned out.

In addition, there is no absolute "wrong." We have gotten so conditioned toward optimizing and being all perfect and shiny that most people seem to think there is one perfect answer, one ideal "right" way forward. Save yourself some time. There isn't. And an unequivocal choice accompanied by focused determination and investment of energy will almost surely work out better than no choice or scattered attempt to do everything.

Choosing is about assessing what has the best chance of achieving your goal based on some combination of what you know and what's unclear. Knowing yourself – your goals, your values, your needs – is a level of self-awareness that creates the most solid foundation possible for making choices.

Once you've made the mental choice, you'll need to commit. Making a commitment technically means that it's impossible to reverse direction. It means eliminating a safety net, which sometimes has to be done in stages and steps, maybe baby steps.

Identifying stages of choosing, or inflections points, is sometimes part of the way forward. Or, as happened in my case, the facts of the situation take on new meaning as time goes on.

When I was a few years into my big, fancy corporate career, I had a great chat with my eighty-seven-year-old grandmother. She asked me to make us both a drink (she'd spent her early married years in a mining camp where my grandfather was an engineer, so she knew how she liked her liquor). I shared my plans for travel, we discussed an offer I'd received to change jobs, and I asked her for advice on a few other decisions I had in front of me. Suddenly, she leaned back and sighed.

"You have so many choices. I don't know how you do it."

I asked her what she meant.

"When I was your age, we didn't have many real choices," she said. "You went to school, you met someone, you got married, you kept house, you had children. That's just the way it was, and no one thought about whether it was good or bad."

I smiled confidently. "Well, isn't it wonderful how times have changed?"

She laughed. "I wouldn't trade places with you for all the tea in China. Your life is way too complicated."

SHARON

Sharon was a young, fast-rising executive in a big company. She made decisions all day long – big ones, expensive ones. She was good at it.

She got a big promotion. With her executive paycheck, she bought her first house.

And she could not commit to hanging a picture on a wall.

She was so afraid of making a "wrong" choice that she made no choices at all. Putting a hole in a wall felt like an irrevocable and major decision. Months after moving in, her pictures were still leaning against walls and sitting in piles on the floor while this brilliant, decisive leader worried – every day – about where things should go.

HOW TO CHOOSE

Most major decisions are best served by a combination of head and heart. The head – the facts and analysis – is usually the easier place to start, but the heart's opinion is often the one that's truer and more connected to your values and what will make you happy. I devised a framework that invites both the head and the heart into the process.

Make three lists: Musts, Reasonables, and Nice-to-Haves.

The Musts are the rock bottom, non-negotiable

aspects of the ideal situation. If it's a job, this list will include salary and location and maybe title or scope of responsibility. If it's a relationship, the Must list might include height, religion, or major interests. A home? Number of bedrooms and neighbourhood location probably fit here. The Must list is short because you are going to say "no" to anything that does not check every box on it. Note: if you find yourself seriously and regularly tempted to move forward with something that does not check all the boxes on the Must list, then take another look at the list. You've probably included something you think ought to be there or that "other people" would expect to see there. If it's not your must, it doesn't belong on the list.

The Reasonables is the list that includes all of the things that would be true in order for the option in question to be perfectly acceptable. The things that take the decision in question from "bad" to "good" but probably not to "great." The criteria and characteristics that make a situation tenable and comfortable but maybe not exciting. The things that probably have to be true in order for you to speak confidently about your decision to anyone who is important to you.

The Nice-to-Haves list – well, here's a place to have some fun. Here's where you put all the crazy, one-in-a-million, never-going-to-happen things that would make something perfect. A loft office with exposed brick and fine art on the walls in a trendy downtown location? Free parking? A home with a wet bar and hot tub? A partner with season's tickets to live theatre and a regular table at a great restaurant? The sky's the limit here. For those of you asking, "Why bother with the crazy list?" it's important to engage your instincts at some stage in any decision-making process. This crazy, out-there list should reflect some of your heart's real desires.

You can ponder over the Musts but don't overthink the others. Try to progress from the analytical to the idealistic. The best decisions connect at every level.

By the way, I've had clients use this list framework to choose outfits, jobs, houses, and, yes, life partners. I can't make this stuff up.

While the lists have proven incredibly useful, both for many clients and for me over the years, there's another filter that can be helpful if there is still doubt: the Timeframe filter.

Ask yourself how you'll feel about your choice right away, in a little while, and in the future. Use any combination of time frames that works for you – I'm a big fan of patterns and rhythm, so I like "ten days, ten months, and ten years," but use any three that work for you given the situation. It's just another way to check in with your instincts once you've used all your brain-based logic.

IF I'D KNOWN THEN WHAT I KNOW NOW

In my coaching practice, I've come to understand that, at least when it comes to "projects," interests, and choices, there are two types of people. I call them "water bugs" and "SCUBA divers."

Water bugs zip across the surface, moving from here to there quickly and never landing in any one spot for long.

SCUBA divers pick a spot and go deep.

Water bugs will see the surface of a great many things and places.

SCUBA divers see and examine one thing at a time in great detail.

Water bugs are most likely to see and take on an abundance of choices, not selecting one at least not for long, and always looking toward the next thing, the better thing.

SCUBA divers will analyze a choice for a long time, possibly not ever finding sufficient information to ensure they feel comfortable about it.

And just to complicate things, there's the dock spider, sitting in the sunshine, waiting for food to come along, not moving.

While this metaphor mostly tells you that I spent a lot of time at a family cottage on a lake, I hope it also illustrates that there is no one perfect way to make decisions – each has its strengths and useful applications.

I've spent a lot of time wishing I was more analytical, that I had the patience and attention span to research options, make lists of criteria, and compare alternatives. That "sleeping on it" and "biding my time" were approaches to decision-making that came naturally to me. The fact is that I'm an instinctive, gut-based decision-maker who loves a variety of options and a little bit of drama just to keep things interesting. I'll sit in one place for a while, but when I move, I move fast. I'm mostly water bug – the more options I see, the more I understand which alternative appeals to me most. My decision-making style makes some of the people around me a little crazy, but I've come to accept that my style works for me. I've also had to accept that on the occasions where my decisions might have indeed benefited from a little more research or time in reflection, I can't deflect the consequences. My decision, my results.

ELIZABETH

I hadn't seen Elizabeth in a while, so when she asked to get together, I was eager to catch up. She is a fellow coach, and I always enjoyed our chats about the profession and things like what we were reading and what conferences and retreats were on our radar.

We greeted each other warmly, and as we were

getting seated, I asked the usual, "How are you? It's been forever."

She jumped right in with her reason for wanting to connect: "I'm getting divorced."

She went on to describe the process of self-reflection she'd undertaken. She'd found her coach-training experience to be profound, and it gave her tools with which to reflect on what was working and not working in her life.

"I take good care of my health. I love my work. I have great relationships with my friends and family. I'm taking care of my finances. But suddenly, I was confronted by something that I'd ignored for a while. I suddenly realized that there was one place in my life where I was totally out of alignment."

She started talking about what had long been missing in her relationship with her husband.

"We see the world differently. We want different things. We want to spend our time differently. We've grown to be quite different than we were when we first got married. Over time, it became clear to me that things weren't going to change, that our relationship was based on an old set of assumptions and values, and that I had become different enough that living by the old assumptions was no longer acceptable to me. None of this was going to change or get better just because I wanted to keep ignoring it."

The differences between them grew to the point where the gap meant something. It evolved from being the source of interesting dinner table conversation to the point where they had nothing in common, including the vision for their life together. Once evaluated, it became clear that choices would have to be made.

When evaluating her choices, Elizabeth had to weigh the value of that level of alignment that she sought against the financial and logistical challenges of divorcing and starting over. When she looked at it that way, she knew what choice would make her happiest in the long term, even if it was the more difficult path in the short term.

REFLECTION

Choosing is hard, but not choosing is, in my view, much more debilitating. Sitting in limbo – not fully in your marriage and not out of it, looking at piles of pictures sitting on the floor rather than displaying them on a wall, letting time pass in a job you don't love but are reluctant to leave – and the non-choices are what will eat away at you.

Assemble your facts, check them against your values, look at yourself in the mirror, and be honest with the person you see reflected back. You're the one who has to live with what you decide – no one else.

7

E – ENERGY: CONSERVE IT, MANAGE IT, AND INVEST IT WISELY

Energy is an equation with some hidden variables. We are usually fairly aware of where we are consciously expending energy – we "do" a lot, and when we're tired, we presume it's because we've "done too much." What we're usually less connected to are those times – and people, and thoughts – where energy is gradually, quietly being depleted. And few people have good practices in place to rebuild energy when supplies are low, let alone before that extreme happens.

Pop quiz: do you let your car get down to fumes before you fill the tank, or do you fill it before you need to? You're probably managing your personal energy similarly. If we take the analogy further, are you putting the best possible fuel in your tank and running yourself in the most efficient way possible? I didn't think so.

Every moment of every day, every activity you undertake, and every person you interact with represents either an addition or a depletion of your energy levels. Nothing is neutral. And while loading yourself up with activities and responsibilities day by day is a great way to get lots done and avoid feeling difficult things, eventually, the crash – the empty tank – does come.

In addition to day-to-day energy levels, you also need to take care of what's known as your "surge capacity." The human adrenal system is designed to withhold a bit of energy just in case of an emergency – encountering a sabre-toothed tiger or living through a world-wide pandemic, just as examples. But if you tap your surge capacity repeatedly without a break and without replenishing it, the crash will be even more dramatic and be harder to recover from.

Consider that we have several operating systems within us, all of which have the potential to use and be sources of energy. The model I like best here is the Quadrinity from the Hoffman Institute. The Hoffman Quadrinity process identifies four aspects of us as humans, all of which require nurturing to function effectively and all of which can be depleted with abuse or lack of attention:

Our physical body responds positively to hydration, exercise, and good food and gets tired when we don't sleep properly or when we consume things that don't nourish us.

Our intellect gets stronger when we challenge it and declines when we aren't intentional about learning and growth and/or when we over-expose it to mindless stimuli.

Our emotions are healthy and helpful when we enjoy good relationships and positive situations and get depleted when we allow negativity around us.

Our spirits are often our least-cared for dimension, responding to quiet reflection and connection with our truest selves and suffering when we don't let them guide and speak to us.

Every aspect of yourself has its own distinct energy needs and uses, and as such, every aspect requires conscious attention and choices. If you're like most people I've worked with, you tend to rely more heavily on one aspect than some of the others (usually the intellectual self), which means that one has gotten used to overriding what the others have to tell you.

The work you'll need to do in this area is to discern which of your energy levels is sufficient or depleted and take actions that will balance them and ensure you're not draining yourself without a plan to replenish regularly. Easier said than done, I'm aware.

Pro tip: if you ever find yourself using the word "should" as you contemplate any course of action, stop and think for a minute. "Should" is the word we use when we feel a sense of obligation, usually externally driven, that conflicts with what we want to do or who we genuinely believe we are. If you're about to proceed with a "should," ask yourself why and be honest. Investing energy in a "should" is almost certainly going to be a depletion.

In the several years that led up to the end of my marriage, I felt stretched so thin, most of the time, it was as if I was hanging on by a thread. I was exhausted, cranky, doing the bare minimum in most categories, and going to bed every night hoping the next day would be better – which it never was, of course.

Once the separation happened, I felt like something had unleashed within me. I had more energy than I'd had in years. I sorted all the administrative and financial details, undertook the renovation of our house, wrote a book, planned big trips, and joined business accelerator programs – and all of this while parenting solo and running a business.

I had wise friends point out that I was on an adrenaline high and that keeping incredibly busy was probably a good way to avoid feeling the normal grief and sadness that follow the end of a marriage.

They weren't wrong.

But they weren't exactly right either. What I was experiencing was the result of a huge shift in available energy that occurred because a big drain had been removed. That said, without recognizing that that's what was going on, I wasn't making conscious choices about where to direct that new energy. And, of course, what I didn't see coming was the fact without initiating some practices that would conserve my energy, I had put myself on a roller coaster that, at some point, was probably going to come to a screeching halt.

What was also happening was that I was focusing on the big, obvious ways to use my energy and was ignoring the tiny drains that were taking place all the time. Like a gradually eroding shoreline, I had things in my life that were sapping my energy small bit by small bit, and I didn't even realize it was happening.

LULU

Doing good work in the world can be fulfilling, but it's got its own brand of challenges. Lulu is a client who forged a career in the not-for-profit world, leading organizations that work to solve social issues. Lulu builds strong relationships with her various boards, donors, staff, and volunteer and community stakeholder groups, and she is generally seen as someone who will work tirelessly for the cause. She has had tremendous passion for her work, deep compassion for those affected by the issues that are the focal point of her organization and understands that with privilege comes responsibility – so she worked. And worked.

Lulu's roles have had her traveling the world, landing her in far-flung locations often for extended periods of time, rendering it challenging for her to sustain relationships of any sort. Even when she's on her home turf, there never seem to be enough hours in the day to satisfy the various audiences to whom she was responsible, particularly on the bare-bones budget typical of a cause-based organization, let alone to see friends or date at all. Over time, Lulu became a. solo act – she was the go-to for everything at work, and yet had little in the way of a support system outside the office.

Knowing she was making a difference on some issues that mattered to her sustained Lulu for a long time – until all of a sudden, it didn't. It didn't happen in a single moment but began shortly after her fortieth birthday when Lulu started to notice that she had just a little less patience for small issues. She felt a little more resentment when asked to do some of the "over and above" things that had always been understood and accepted. She needed to sleep more, was a bit more reluctant to get on a plane, and found herself less likely to work late at the office. The changes were subtle, at least at first, so it took a long-overdue coaching session for Lulu to reflect on how she was feeling. And what she realized was that, after a couple of decades of doing for others, she'd hit a wall.

HOW TO MANAGE YOUR ENERGY

What gives you energy, or puts gas in your personal metaphorical tank? What drains it? Getting conscious about your inflows and outflows of energy – the "net gain or net drain" – has to happen before you can make choices that better support you. Here are several approaches and exercises that I use both myself and with clients. In this realm, I think more tools are better.

The Small Stuff

When I was in my first coach training program, we learned some exercises that were designed to identify the things that were getting in the way of us living happy, fulfilling lives. And spoiler alert: some of the barriers to happiness and ease are ridiculously small. Here's a simple tool to start with: the premise here is that every moment and interaction in your day has the potential to either contribute positive energy or drain it – to be a plus or a minus. In this case, you will be focusing, at least to begin with, on the small drains, the minuses. Your task is to make a list of all of them, every last loose end, not-done thing, broken thing, ill-fitting thing, dirty thing – all of it. Another spoiler alert: once you've built this list, your assignment is going to be to deal with everything on it. Every last item. Eradicated. Imagine.

As an example, you know those cute little throw pillows you use to make your bed look nice? I went through a period of time where the ruffle on one side of one of the pillows had gotten detached. Every time I made the bed and picked up that pillow, I had a little moment of "yuck, I should fix that," a tiny little daily negative – an energy drain – a minus. For about a year. When I did this exercise and included the throw pillow on the list, I had to fix it, which took exactly three minutes. Do the math – a year of daily negatives turned into a future of daily positives with an investment of three minutes. Once I fixed the pillow, when I picked it up every day to put it on the bed, I no longer had the "yuck" thought; I instead would look at it and think, "Oh, that looks nice." A positive. Your assignment here is to make that list – if you're normal, you could get to a hundred little things pretty easily – and then one by one, start fixing or dealing with them. Dirty car? Get it washed. Burned out light bulb or missing button? Replace it, attach it, deal with it. You get the idea. But be aware – eventually, these things are probably going to get harder and more expensive to fix satisfactorily, but as you notice the change in your energy level, you might start to accept that those investments are worth it.

Choose Your Reactions

In the classic personal development book "7 Habits of Highly Effective People" by Stephen R. Covey, there is a model that I use regularly with clients because it's deceptively simple and quite powerful called the Circle of Influence. It's a graphic that looks like a donut and illustrates where you're best to place your focus based on where you've got the greatest opportunity to create change or have an impact.

In the inside circle are the things over which you've got maximum control – your actions and choices are pretty much all that fits here. The outer circle holds the things that are going to happen no matter what you do. The weather? Outer circle. Your choice of wardrobe for the day? Inside circle. Your reaction to the weather? Inside circle. Yes, that's right – the place you've got the greatest ability to exert influence and make better choices is in your reactions to events and the behaviours you choose as a result of those choices.

In the later part of my corporate career, I got transferred to Dallas, Texas. The day I arrived, there was a tornado that killed nine people, and it rained for a couple of weeks after that pretty consistently. I went back home to attend a wedding and happened to be seated next to a former colleague who I knew had lived in Dallas for a couple of years. I complained about the terrible weather for a bit until he interrupted me with a wise suggestion: "When it rains, put on your bathing suit and wash your car."

We've all got limits on our energy, time, and attention. Why not place our focus on the situations and issues where we can move the needle?

ROIEE

This tool shortcuts the one above and is focused on your emotional self – the aspect of you that often feels like it's hardest to manage. These days, it takes about three seconds on social media to get your blood pressure rising. Before you engage, there, anywhere, or with anyone, ask yourself this question: What will be the return on my investment of emotional energy here? The ROIEE is the simplest way I've found to get people to check themselves before getting irate or involved in things that ultimately either won't matter much or that they won't be able to influence at all.

Human Energy Vampires and the Unequivocal No

As I mentioned earlier, one of the often overlooked and almost always ignored drains of energy are the people who surround you. How often do you agree to an event or an invitation that you know will drain you or engage in a conversation you later wished you'd been able to avoid?

A client recently asked me for advice about how to respond to an invitation that she didn't want to accept but felt she "should." Remember, the word "should" is a red flag in any situation. She had a vague sense of obligation but a much clearer understanding that the event in question, with the people involved, would not be something she'd enjoy. I offered up the question about "net gain or net drain" of energy. She said she saw the proverbial light bulb go on – the event would most certainly be a net drain, and since she had no active contribution to make or requirement to be there, it became clear that she needed to decline. Then, we got to work on her language for doing just that.

"No" is a perfectly acceptable response to an invitation or a request of any variety. Be polite, be kind, but be firm if you are clear that the idea in question will deplete you. Your ability to say no without justifying your decisions might be one of the least developed but most powerful tools women can learn.

Mindfulness

Your ability to employ most of the above, not to mention your ability to be conscious about your energy in general, will be vastly enhanced with one simple practice added to your life. Mindfulness –

which, for simplicity, I'll define as "non-judgmental attention to the current moment" – has enjoyed a lot of recent buzz for good reasons. Even the simplest, briefest regular mindfulness practice can reduce stress, improve focus, enhance decision-making, regulate emotions, and support improved sleep. Not bad for something that can be done in ten minutes a day, right?

Regular mindfulness practice is as effective as it's reported to be because it changes the physiology of the brain. I'm not going to attempt to educate you on the science here – there are legions of books and articles that can help you learn all of that – but I will assure you that the reports are true. The one key, though, is regular practice. Consistency is powerful in most things. For mindfulness practice, that's particularly true.

You can start to enjoy the benefits of mindfulness practice in ten minutes a day counting your breath. But don't just count it in a linear way; try counting it from one to ten and then from ten to one. This ensures you'll keep your attention on the breath, whereas if you counted from one to some indefinite point, you'd quickly shift into autopilot.

The key to success in a mindfulness practice is to accept that your attention will wander. When it does, and you realize it, just shift back to counting. And do it again tomorrow. Within about two weeks, you'll start to feel the effects – you'll be just a little more able to pause before agreeing, take a breath before replying, listen to your instincts, and give a bit of thought before committing.

IF I'D KNOWN THEN WHAT I KNOW NOW

I'm masterful at staying busy, prioritizing everything from kids to clients and even housecleaning over getting quiet and connecting to myself at a deep level. And I'm good at living up to the "strong, capable, reliable, responsible, and yes, helpful" reputation I seem to have cultivated over the years.

One of the best and worst things about what I do for a living, though, is that I'm regularly confronted with my own work to do and a need to feel a sense of integrity when I'm suggesting things to my clients. No matter how much I believed in the importance of mindfulness, if I wasn't prepared to walk the talk, I didn't feel comfortable preaching about it to my clients. The tools I've outlined above have, over time, become fundamental to how I make choices about what I take on, who I spend time with, and what I allow to occupy my attention.

Of course, over time, I've noticed that I sleep better, I laugh more often, I have time for the things and people who I value, and generally have confidence that most of my choices are supportive rather than depleting. I'm not perfect, by any stretch, and I can get side-tracked every now and again, but I'm certainly more conscious about when I'm heading toward a direction that will require some course-correction.

Or, as my client Max shared, "In a strange way, I think our work together has even helped my golf game."

KRISTOFFER

I hesitated to include a story about a man's strategies and experiences in a book targeted to women because, for the most part, I think our worldviews are pretty different, especially related to the ideas I'm concerned with here regarding overwhelm, overload, and energy management. But there's a great principle to be understood from this example, so bear with me.

I met Kristoffer at the entrepreneurial immersion I attended when I was simultaneously recovering from the divorce and writing my first book. KC, as he's known, was a husband, a thirty-something father of three, a regional sales leader for a digital media company, a performing rock musician, and a marathon runner, and he was attempting to build a side hustle so he could eventually leave his corporate gig. I think it's understandable that, as I was getting to know him and appreciate everything that he was up to, I asked, "How on earth do you do it all?"

His unequivocal answer: meditation.

KC had his struggles with mood swings, people-pleasing, water bugging, and taking on too many projects, all of which eventually forced him to confront what was working and not working in his life. Through a series of events that he couldn't ignore, he connected with the work of Parmahansa Yogananda and undertook the study of Kriya yoga. As is his way, he jumped in with both feet, and most days since he began, he has done about an hour of sitting meditation, often twice a day.

KC credits meditation with supporting his ability to focus, to prioritize based on what's important, to be more present with his family, and to live a healthier life. Or, as he likes to say, "None of this gets done without meditation."

Make no mistake, though, meditation or any form of mindfulness or reflective practice is not a cure-all, nor is it a guarantee that you won't backslide every now and again. Or, as KC's amazing wife, Gayle, pointed out to him one morning while he was having the kind of meltdown he has come to refer to as a "mantrum," "For a guy who meditates as much as you do, you're sure acting like a turd right now."

REFLECTION

It took a while, but I've come to not only accept some form of mindfulness practice as being essential to a conscious, peaceful, intentional, thriving life,

I've progressed such that I actively seek out opportunities for silence and reflection. Sometimes it's a formal sitting practice, but at other times, it's what my friend Emiliya Zhivotovskaya, wise teacher of many things including positive psychology, refers to as "a million mindful moments."

Managing your energy takes conscious effort and intention and is going to be best done when you are crystal clear about what – and who – creates the big and small "plus" moments for you.

8

I – INITIATE. GO AFTER WHAT YOU NEED

The paradox of being a "strong" woman is that you are both perfectly capable of taking care of yourself and desperately hopeful that you don't always have to. And if you've successfully created the "strong" persona, those that know you probably think you've got everything handled.

When you make or undergo a change in your life – or even if you haven't changed anything, but you've dropped into a comfortable but unsatisfying routine – you have to re-craft your support structures, your community, and, well, everything. You have to tell people you're out there and ask for what you want.

The biggest temptation is to hunker down, retreat, protect yourself, and lick your wounds.

That is, at best, a short-term strategy.

In fact, what you have to do as soon as you realize there's an issue is start reaching out.

Because if you don't, two things will happen: you'll get into the habit of isolating, and people will forget about you. In order to make sure that neither of those things happens, you're the one who's going to have to dig deep and get vulnerable enough to speak up and ask for what you need.

You'll need infrastructure – a dream team of people you can call on for specific things. You'll also need emotional connections and support, which is not the same as the kind of tactical and logistics help that will help you juggle all of your responsibilities.

You need the courage to ask for what you need, and you need community.

Community is critical and magical, but real community doesn't just happen. To be surrounded by people who not only care but who will tell you the truth, who have your best interests at heart even when it's not what you want to hear, who are as able to give as to receive for themselves, who are diverse enough to have an array of perspectives as well as the willingness and ability to play different roles, that's magic and does not form by accident. Although, I do believe that if you put yourself on a good path, some happy accidents might just occur.

By the way, asking and initiating don't have to be about big things. I heard a great story about a man and a woman, colleagues on a business trip, who illustrated this point beautifully. After they had checked into their hotel and gotten settled in their rooms, they met in the hotel bar. The woman expressed delight at her lovely room but a tinge of disappointment that there was no nice fluffy robe in the bathroom. The man said he'd noticed the same thing, so he called down to the concierge, and they had one delivered a few minutes later.

If you don't ask, you don't get.

While I'm not very educated about astrology, I do know that there are some commonly held understandings of the characteristics that come with being born under a particular sun sign. I'm a Leo, which, as I understand it, means I'm pretty sure I'm the centre of the universe.

Imagine my chagrin when, as I began my new phase of life as a solo person and single parent, I found myself home alone, well, always and handling everything without sympathetic ears, shared glasses of wine, or offers of carpools and playdates. No invitations to dinners, few dates (don't get me started), no holiday parties or celebratory events, no one checking up on me to see how I was doing or if I needed anything. No offers to help me with my kids or questions about if I needed anything when a neighbour ran to the store. No one reaching out. At all. And while I realized I would have to make an effort, I was so overwhelmed and was juggling so many things that I had a hard time getting organized enough to extend invitations to others. I did it every once in a while – a Christmas drinks party, the occasional dinner gathering – but reciprocal invitations rarely came, so I decided the effort wasn't worth it.

No matter how logically I could rationalize the fact that I didn't have a long line up of well-wishers and helpful friends at my door, I still felt lonely and resentful. Which spirals quickly in an unattractive way – nobody wants to spend time with someone who's feeling sorry for themselves. Difficult events aren't contagious, but misery sort of is.

And while I do understand that getting divorced implies that you're accepting the role of solo everything, it still seemed strange that I had what I thought was a strong community of neighbours and friends and yet – crickets.

This absence of infrastructure and community that began as a source of self-pity and frustration quickly became a mystery that I had to unravel. If it was just me, I needed to know. If there was a bigger problem, I wanted to understand and hopefully solve it, not just for myself but for other women like me.

Pop quiz: How many other people's support systems are you a part of? Did you agree to be there? Would those people willingly be part of yours? While life isn't best run via a scorecard, if you're contributing more than you're – yes – receiving, you might want to take a look at where your community activities are working or not.

ANGELA

Angela is a single mother and business owner in her early forties. While she was married, she and her husband and daughter moved cities several times, never staying long enough anywhere to put down deep roots. After going through a painful and messy divorce, Angela made a conscious choice to move with her daughter back to the large city where she'd spent much of her adult life before getting married.

"I wanted to tuck back into that community that I loved so much. I wanted to be able to see friends, do fun things, and feel like I had a support system, so I didn't feel alone."

Angela reached out to me in early July, about a year after she'd moved back to that beloved city.

"Here I am, it's Fourth of July weekend, and do you think I've had even one invitation to a celebration?"

She had reconnected with many old friends in the year she'd been back yet was still finding that she was the one who was having to initiate the get-togethers.

By simply showing up, being in the same place, and sharing the story of the rough road she'd travelled since she'd left, Angela presumed people would be excited to see her and would extend invitations and welcome her back into their circles. In turn, the friends presumed that she was recovering from the divorce and the move and transitioning to being a single parent and that she'd reach out when she was ready.

Stalemate.

EXERCISE

Societally, we have developed a bit of a twisted relationship with obligations and guilt. I believe that if I could develop one new skill that would make a big difference in how most people communicate, it would be the skill of making a request. If you're going to start asking people for what you need, you're going to have to know how to do it in an effective way. And that starts with understanding what a request is. (Note: in my view "request" and "invitation" can be handled the same way).

A request makes a clear ask and has three clear, equally acceptable options for response. Here's how it works.

Friend making a request of me: "Would you like to come for dinner this evening?"

When someone makes an authentic request – not a demand cloaked innocuously, not a passive-aggressive attempt to create guilt, but a real request – the recipient has three legitimate responses: accept, decline, or counter offer.

In the above case, here are my possible responses:

Accept: "I'd be delighted. What shall I bring?"

Decline: "Unfortunately, I'm not available." (Note: No explanation is necessary. It doesn't matter why you're not available – even if you're planning an evening in your pyjamas with a good book, your reason is no one else's business).

Counteroffer: "This evening doesn't work, but how about lunch tomorrow?"

Now imagine you're going to ask for what you need and want. One of the issues I've heard is that it's hard to know how to help a strong, smart, capable woman. It's up to us to make the "specific ask." We need to make it easier for people to help us. Oh, and by the way, most people do want to help. They usually don't think they know how, or they have great intentions but forget to follow through. Yes, let's make it easier for them.

Start small and be precise. Let's say you could use some help with mid-week grocery odds and ends. Your ask of a neighbour might be something like, "If I work with your schedule, limit my ask to five items or less, and give you cash upfront, could you pick up a few things for me next time you're at the grocery store?"

They might say yes.

They might say not this week, but maybe next.

And they might say no.

Whichever it is, the act of asking is good exercise. And their response to you does not validate or judge you as a human being. If you get what you need, great. If not, ask if there's another option, or move on to another person. But understand that no one can read your mind, most people think you're doing just fine, and if you want help, you're the one who's going to have to come right out and ask for it.

IF I'D KNOWN THEN WHAT I KNOW NOW

As I was collecting stories for this book, I found myself particularly curious about this aspect of being strong. Do other women have similar experiences? Do other women struggle to get what they need, or was it just me? I posted a question on social media.

Turns out, it's not just me (phew). Do other women feel alone and struggle to get what they need? Yes. Vehemently, unequivocally yes. In the space of a couple of hours, more than fifty women commented on the post. Many who responded were single mothers who felt particularly lonely and particularly overwhelmed with responsibilities, but beyond that, there was a common thread of having some sort of specific, significantly life-shifting experience that resulted in a feeling of isolation – the Accidental Alpha phenomenon. Grief, illness, caregiving, financial upheaval – women who were deep in their unique experiences felt like they had no one to turn to and were hurt that no one thought to ask if they needed support.

What was particularly interesting, especially given recent economic trends toward entrepreneurship and self-employment, was that women business owners who were also the ones carrying the responsibility for their families were feeling particularly alone and overwhelmed. Being the go-to for all of the people in both work and family systems was described as massively tiring and isolating.

When it comes to community, one of the best things to happen to me was equally a result of smart thinking on my part and serendipitous events created by others. That entrepreneurial immersion program I joined connected me to a small number of other people who shared my personal values of learning, contribution, and community. A year or so after I first met this group, the founder Jonathan Fields and his wife, Stephanie, decided to create a crazy thing that sounded too good to be true: summer camp for grown-ups. Camp Good Life Project, or Camp GLP as it's come to be known, brought several of us from that first immersion together with over four hundred like-minded people from around the world for three and a half days of play, creativity, fun, S'mores, singing, late nights, workshops, and inspiration. It's a group of people who stay connected to this day, even though the last Camp event was over two years ago, and who are as likely to share their favourite brands of glitter and best kale recipes as they are to ask for help processing deep grief or business disasters. It's come to be widely accepted that wherever you are in the world, if you call for a GLP meet-up, you'll get one and that if you need anything at all, you just ask the group, and if someone is able to help, they will, no questions asked. It's special.

MARY

Mary became a single parent when her kids were pretty young, and she quickly learned that taking care of herself landed at the bottom of the list most days. But she also knew that if she was to function at all in her simultaneously demanding roles of mother and management consultant, she'd have to figure out how to take care of herself.

She brought this issue to a coaching session, and we brainstormed a bit. We talked about asking for help. She got creative.

Mary's next-door neighbour was an early riser and liked to enjoy his morning coffee and the newspaper on his front porch shortly after sunrise. Mary liked the peace of the mornings before her kids were up and occasionally had the chance to chat with the neighbour. One day, she mentioned that she was struggling to figure out how to get some exercise. She made a request of the neighbour: would he allow her to bring the baby monitor out onto the front porch and leave it where he could hear it while she went for a run? She made it clear that the kids normally slept for another hour beyond when she'd be doing the run and that if the neighbour heard anything, he could send her a message on her phone, and she'd come back right away. She also let him know that if he wasn't comfortable with the idea, it was no problem at all. Of course, he agreed, and Mary now was able to get out for a short run several mornings a week.

We sometimes overestimate the difficulty and complexity of our challenges. In fact, sometimes, what we need is just a tiny bit of simple help. Mary's situation proved that people are generally willing to help, especially if you are specific and modest in your request.

If you don't ask, you won't get. Or, as attributed to Wayne Gretzky, "You miss 100 percent of the shots you never take."

REFLECTION

Taking ownership of your needs and interests starts with getting clear on what those needs and interests are. Then comes what seems to be the challenging part: asking. Asking is hard, but not asking and suffering is worse. And eventually, asking will lead you to a life that feels more like it might belong to you. Let's go there.

9

V – VOICE. DISCOVER AND EXPRESS WHO YOU ARE

When your context changes, your operating principles – the way you show up and go through life – might need to be examined. If you take on change in one area of your life and don't consider whether other things might need a shakeup, you are at the least missing an opportunity and possibly creating a situation where the various component parts of your life don't work well together. And if you're coming into this process with only a vague sense that your life isn't working and you continue as you've been going, I promise you'll get pretty much what you've gotten so far. Even if most days most things in your life seem to be working pretty well, it's still a great idea to check in with yourself and see whether there are ways you could be honouring yourself better or more consistently than you are.

You have an inner voice – a guide or instinct that tells you what makes you happy, what feels right, what choices to make, and even what people to spend time with. But extended periods of caregiving, responsibility, overwhelm, and the unfortunate habit of putting yourself last means that, over time, your inner voice – your intuition – is hard to hear. If you're going to change how you're approaching your life, getting better at listening to that voice (which is your ultimate RECEIVE mechanism) will be critical, as will allowing yourself to show up in the world expressing what that voice tells you.

There was a time when I knew how to speak up for what I believed in.

The summer I was ten years old, we were at our family cottage and, as happened every summer, my grandparents came for a weekend.

That particular weekend happened to coincide with a period of time when my mother had attempted, once again, to give up smoking.

As the grown-ups were enjoying their cocktails, I overheard my father tell my mother something along the lines that he'd prefer she started smoking again because she was cranky.

I found this outrageous and loudly pronounced that I would never smoke. My father not only agreed that I should never start, but offered to buy me a mink coat (a desirable prize back in those days, and remember, the cocktails were flowing) on my eighteenth birthday if I got to that point in my life without having taken up the habit.

I promptly wrote up a contract confirming the deal. He and I both signed it, and I got my grandfather to witness it.

I've still got the paper contract. And on my eighteenth birthday, I received the cash value of a mink coat.

As I reflect on that day, it's clear to me that I instinctively knew what I believed, was courageous enough to speak it even in the face of opposing views (and from authority figures), could recognize an opportunity, and was astute enough to understand that some formal accountability was important.

There are at least two things that I find particularly interesting about this story. First, I ended up in the business of challenging people to do better and then holding them to their commitments – who could have seen that coming? And second, I don't recall feeling nervous, uncertain, or in any way vulnerable as I took a strong stand in that moment.

I can't help but wonder when that courage dissipated.

TALA

Tala is a beautiful, intelligent, modern Asian woman. Highly educated, ambitious, and fearless, she graduated from a top business school and jumped into a career in consulting with every intention of running the firm one day.

At the same time, Tala has strong traditional roots. She's a good daughter and sister and considers herself grounded in and supported by her culture's values.

The combination of the modern and traditional might seem odd or uncommon, but it's exactly what makes Tala who she is in every real and meaningful way, and she's always been crystal clear that she is both.

For the longest time, Tala wasn't sure she'd ever meet someone who shared her traditional values and could also appreciate her modern sensibilities and ambitions. Yet, amazingly enough, she discovered romance with a man who was similarly rooted in his traditional upbringing, who was also succeeding in high-tech business.

Their wedding was an extraordinary celebration in all the traditional ways, and they set up a home together.

The signs were there from the beginning, Tala says, but she didn't want to see them.

It seemed that while she and her husband each had a foot in both modern and traditional worlds, she was leaning toward the more modern life, whereas he was tipping quickly toward the traditional ways, at least at home. She felt strongly about equality while he preferred to be served, taken care of, and retain control of major decisions.

She found herself pulled and conflicted; she loved her career but felt honour-bound to uphold the commitment she'd made to be a good wife.

As time went on, Tala grew more certain that she could both succeed at her career and honour her culture and family but that she didn't have a partner who saw things the same way. Once she reflected on what she wanted and who she wanted to be in a marriage, she saw that their differences were irreconcilable. Although she feared disappointing her parents, when she shared her issues with them, she discovered that they, too, saw both sides of her and truly just wanted her to be happy.

Tala and her traditional husband divorced within a year of being married. Once she'd made that decision, she knew she might be choosing to be alone, but that was a possibility she accepted. As it turns out, releasing herself from a situation where she couldn't truly be herself gave her the freedom to blossom and find out who she is in the world. She's gone on to make a major geographic move, build a successful business rooted in all of who she authentically is, and has met and married a man who honours all of her.

HOW TO FIND YOUR VOICE

I find that when I'm challenging clients to get in touch with a deeper, maybe long-hidden aspect of themselves, it's helpful to get them doing things that they wouldn't normally do – arts and crafts, movement, mixing up their routine, or anything that ensures their brain doesn't drop into normal patterns. With that in mind, here are a few things you might try to see where a long-silent voice might emerge.

Photo Shopping

Go looking for photos in as many different subject matters and genres as possible – and I mean hundreds. It's best to shop a big magazine rack if you can, but if that's not possible, then Pinterest can work. The goal here is to momentarily expose yourself to a massive range of visual stimuli and to just notice what you connect with. I know that if I don't filter or overthink it, I'll gravitate toward textile arts, colourful French and Italian villages, and rustic antique furniture. Once you've gathered a big selection, without overthinking, go through them and see whether there are any clusters or patterns or common themes.

Take a Test

There are a few tests out there that can give you some insight that runs a bit deeper than the standard "What colour are you?" or "What four letters describe you?" kinds of things. There are two that I like – one is the Sparketype, which distills your individual interests, aptitudes, and motivations into a "type" that describes the essential DNA of your ideal work (mine is Advisor Warrior, which makes perfect sense for a professional coach who has blazed a few trails in the field). Another is the Highlands Ability Battery, which assesses your natural aptitudes across a wide array of categories that you wouldn't normally consider (who knew I had perfect rhythmic memory, perfect tonal memory, and perfect pitch?).

Phone a Friend

Well, maybe not phone, but there are people in your life who know you well, and who have opinions. Make a list of twenty people who know you well – well enough to tell you their real opinion and well enough to know you beneath the surface of what you do for a living or whose parent you are. Craft a note to the list, asking them something along the lines of, "If you could see me doing anything at all with my life, with no barriers or limitations, what would you see me doing?" Or, "If you could see me taking up a new hobby or personal interest..." Or, "If you could see me living anywhere in the world..." You get the idea. Ask one broad, totally open-ended question, and you might be amazed at what you get. One fun example was the client who was an account manager in an ad agency in a big city who did this when she was trying to figure out her career direction – twelve out of twenty respondents, including her grandmother, said some variation of "Forest Ranger." Coincidence? I don't think so.

Find your Flow

There have been times in your life when you have been lit up, in "the zone," loving what you're doing and feeling positive and energized even if you were working hard or confronting big challenges. Sit down with pen and paper and come up with about half a dozen of those moments in your life – young, old, personal, professional – when and where doesn't matter. Reconnect with the feelings you had in those moments. Now sit back and take a look – are there any common themes or through lines?

Try Something New

You don't know what you don't know. What if glass art, hang-gliding, weightlifting, tap dancing, or refinishing furniture unleashes something in you?

How will you know where and how you most love to express yourself if you don't experiment with new things? The idea here is to do just that – try something new. The least risky way into this mindset-shifting practice is to take one day and do everything differently than you would do it normally. Get out of bed on a different side, eat breakfast before you shower, take public transit rather than driving, dig back into the closet for that outfit you haven't worn in forever – in every moment of one full day, ask yourself, "Did I do this yesterday?" and if the answer is "yes," then do it differently or do something else. The goal is to stimulate your brain differently – our neural pathways get pretty deeply formed unless we expose them to new things. And who knows, you may be like the executive client of mine who did this and, as she reported on her day, her final comment was, "Oh, I wore thong underwear to work. I'm not sure it's the way to go, but it sure gave me a different perspective on my day."

The objective here isn't to use a magazine sort or online test to drive you toward a wholesale life change – although if that kind of clarity emerges, go for it. Rather, I'm suggesting undertaking some activities and processes that get you reconnected to your unique voice, your keen interests, and your happiest moments. Once you've uncovered a few of those, ask yourself the question, "How can I get more of this in my life?" I know that once I learned that I had all of these oddly overdeveloped musical skills (in spite of abandoning piano lessons as a teenager), I realized that just having music playing at home and in my office more often gave me a sense of peace that I didn't even know had been missing.

JANE

By the time Jane's two boys were four and six, she could barely recognize herself. She felt depressed, dull, overweight, and generally uninspired by who she was and where her life was going. Her marriage was okay, her boys were fine, and they lived in a nice house in a lovely community – all the boxes were ticked, but still, she felt deeply unsettled and dissatisfied.

Jane had gone to school to be an early childhood educator. She found the work enjoyable enough, but over time, it felt like she was just going through the motions – not to mention that once she'd had kids, she found she didn't want to be taking care of other people's children all day.

She made a few attempts to get back into shape, but nothing appealed enough to spur a real habit or commitment to her health. She felt purposeless and unfulfilled. She grew more and more despondent.

Then one day, she saw that a new fitness centre had opened not too far from her home. It wasn't just a regular gym; the sign said, "Pole Dancing for Fitness."

In her youth, Jane was a tap and jazz dancer and a performer. Like many young adults who danced recreationally, as soon as she turned eighteen, her attention turned toward becoming responsible and career-minded. She missed the feeling of dance – but on a pole? Not in a million years. However, a friend encouraged her to try it, and she skeptically went to a first class where her life changed forever.

Jane loved pole dancing. She found the music, the femininity of the shapes you could form with your body, the sensuality of the movements, the costumes, and the community of bold, confident, creative, fully self-expressed women in the studio lit her up.

She attended classes regularly. She took to pole dancing immediately, and her body started to respond. She got stronger, fitter, healthier, and happier. Her self-confidence grew. She'd found her "thing."

Over time, Jane went from being a regular student to a competitor, to performing in shows and events, and then to becoming a teacher.

Jane eventually built her own pole dancing studio and created a business that helped thousands of women have the same liberating, confidence-building experience that she'd had. It wasn't all glitter and sequins, though. Jane learned along the way that, while pole dancing felt like the perfect expression of who she was, not everyone felt that similarly. Jane has had to combat hecklers in event crowds and vandals at her studio.

Still, Jane knows without question that pole dancing has given her something that nothing else could have; it's given her self-confidence, health, happiness, and a clear, unique voice that she continues to use to help women feel stronger and more confident with who they are.

REFLECTION

Getting clear on who you are, particularly in the face of change, not to mention the expectations and comfort levels of the people around you, is hard. Weeding through your self-talk, your commitments, and your default tendency to put your interests and fulfilment at the bottom of your priority list takes courage and determination. What's clear to me, though, is that the minute you do exactly that, the minute you step into something that you love that lights you up and energizes you, the beneficial ripple into the rest of your life is worth any bumps you encounter in the process. Being more of who you are and doing more of what you love ultimately makes life easier. Or, at least, it's a good foundation upon which to create the systems and practices that you'll be able to sustain that do create more ease.

10

E – EASE CREATE AN EASIER LIFE FOR YOURSELF

As a strong woman, you have a tendency to take on too much, to struggle alone, and to focus on what's not done or done poorly rather than on what progress has been made. You put other people and other people's priorities first to ensure you don't disappoint. You generally are terrible at celebrating your accomplishments and are reluctant to relinquish control for fear that bad things will happen. What bad things, exactly? I don't know about you, but I'm no longer clear about what I've been so afraid of.

But what if you were to celebrate progress and improvement over time?

What if you were to focus on one or two important things?

What if you were to trust yourself and your intuition to guide you toward priorities and choices?

And what if you were more willing to accept help and tolerate imperfection for the sake of lightening your load?

Rather than New Year's resolutions, I've long preferred the practice of choosing a word to be my guideline for a year. I find that having a simple theme grounds me and gives me a litmus test against which to check decisions and ideas. For example, if my word for the year is "health," it helps me choose many things – what to learn about, how to spend my time and money, and probably most importantly and usefully, what kinds of things to not do, or at least do less of.

For several years in a row, as I struggled to get my life on track and dig myself out of the overwhelming financial hole I'd fallen into post-divorce, I found myself choosing the word "ease." In fact, it was in a conversation with my good friend, an extraordinary coach herself, Cynthia Morris, when I connected with this desire for the elusive feeling of ease.

It spanned all the major categories. Financial ease – not having to worry about money. Physical ease – being at the right weight and in good shape. Logistical ease – not feeling as if I was spinning a million plates all at once. It just meant that at the time, my life felt much more difficult than I wanted it to be and thought it ought to or needed to be, and I needed to focus in order to create it differently.

I knew I didn't have aspirations – at least not at that time – to earn millions, gain massive fame, or run marathons. My goals were modest; all centred around climbing up out of the trough I felt I'd been in and lightening the load of worry and fear that I'd been carrying for what felt like forever. Mostly, I just wanted to not have to be so damn strong and resilient all the time.

So, ease. Not a joy ride, not a luxury trip, but most things working pretty well and minimal or only occasional struggles. Energy directed toward the things that will respond to it and not wasted on things where it won't pay back. Systems and infrastructure set up to support me, rather than require me to expend repetitive or unnecessary effort. Ease.

AN EASIER HOUSE

When I split from my kids' dad, I made a commitment to inflict as little change as possible on them. To that end, I took on a massive mortgage in order to keep them in their childhood home in the neighbourhood with all of their friends rather than uproot them in the midst of all of the other upheaval.

It was beyond tough for those first five or six years, paying spousal support, covering all of the household expenses, and carrying that beast of a debt. But it was what I had decided, and remember, I'm strong, so I soldiered on.

Until one day – I still can't recall what prompted it – it dawned on me that maybe there was another way. Maybe moving – downsizing – wouldn't be terrible. Maybe the fact that my kids were a few years older than they'd been when all the change happened meant something. Maybe my assumptions about what we all needed could be checked and updated.

And maybe making a change that would make my life easier would, in fact, be the best thing for my kids.

One evening, over dinner, I tentatively broached the subject.

"I was thinking, what if we maybe took a look around for a different house? Maybe one closer to school? Maybe one that's a little newer than this one? A bit smaller, so there wouldn't be so many chores and odd jobs and things that need repairing all the time?"

I got my older son at "closer to school." "I'd love to be able to sleep in a bit more in the mornings instead of having such a long walk."

I got my younger son at "newer, and less to do." "I hate old things. I'd love to live somewhere where everything was new and worked all the time."

We talked about what would have to be true in order for moving to appeal to all of us. A specific maximum distance from school. Space for them to have friends over. Minimal driveway shoveling and lawn care required. And, for me, at least, a price point that would relieve me of some of the mortgage debt I'd taken on.

It turned out that while my original commitment had been well-intentioned and probably the right decision at the time, things had changed, and the reasons for taking on the financial load and keeping the kids in their childhood home no longer made as much sense as they first did. But I'd been so focused on "handling" the choice I'd made that I hadn't been able to see that there was, in fact, an option that would allow me more ease. This is a great example of being so close to a problem that you can't see when it's not the same problem anymore.

EXERCISE

Finding ease doesn't have, at least in my experience, one access point or magical exercise that transforms you. Rather, it's conscious attention to where you're feeling stress and what "easier" would feel like. It's saying "no" when that's what you want to say. It's streamlining, simplifying, and giving yourself time to breathe.

Ask yourself some of the following questions:

Where are your stress points?

What are you attached to?

Where do you have control? Influence? Neither?

Where are you resisting an alternative that might offer you some ease?

What rules have you set for yourself that are, in fact, creating stress and struggle?

What is depleting you?

What would help you sleep more easily?

What can you get rid of? Let go of?

What are you grateful for?

WHAT I LEARNED

Accepting – or, more actively, inviting – ease into your life is in and of itself an exercise in receiving.

I have enough mystics and spiritual leaders in my life to know better than to question why things fall into place once you get your intentions and asks lined up. In the case of the idea of moving house, once I'd accepted the idea that a move would create more ease, the boys and I had a longer conversation about what the right house would look like, and we began attending open house events in the desired area so we could fine-tune our specifications.

We didn't set a firm timeline but rather agreed that we'd know it when we found it and that, in the meantime, we should get our current house ready so we could act quickly when we found the right thing. To that end, I was doing some work in the front yard one day when my next-door neighbour appeared on her front porch. We started chatting, and I told her what we were planning – that we had a sense of what we were looking for and that we had started the process. She asked for details, and I shared some of the key items on our list.

She went quiet with an odd look on her face.

"Have I ever introduced you to my brother?"

Turns out, her brother was twenty-four hours away from putting a "For Sale" sign on a house that was in the exact neighbourhood we were looking for, at the right price, and sounded like it met most of our other criteria. In spite of it sounding too good to be true, we arranged to go and visit, me with healthy skepticism and the boys with their lists of requirements.

Crazily enough, it was perfect. It met all of our Musts, all of our Reasonables, and a couple of our Nice-to-Haves, plus a couple of things that never occurred to us to ask for. (Recently renovated gourmet kitchen, anyone? Interior paint less than a month old in exactly the right colours? Back door entrance direct to the basement for teenager access? I couldn't make this stuff up).

With an invitation for ease, a clear list of decision-making criteria, and a willingness to accept magic when it appeared, we signed the deal and moved in a month later. And all it took was being clear on what I – we – wanted, being willing to ask for it, and then paying attention when it showed up right under my nose.

DIMPLE

Dimple is a single, working mother of three boys. That statement alone would entitle her to show up a little harried and disorganized, and if she confessed to struggling at all, everyone would understand.

But most of the time, Dimple is smiling, peaceful, and serene. How does she do it?

Dimple swears by rituals and self-care.

Prior to knowing Dimple, I believed that rituals were rigid, time-consuming, and, if truth be told, probably boring or religious. But what Dimple has helped me understand is that when you think of rituals differently, when you think of them as practices that are simple and additive and provide support, well, they become the difference between surviving and thriving.

Dimple's journey into adopting rituals started when her kids were young, and she was feeling physically depleted, out of shape, and like her time was out of her control. She began by carving out a half-hour every day to exercise. She managed to stick with that new routine long enough to start feeling better, so she added on, one small step at a time, over time.

Eventually, as Dimple expanded and formalized

her daily rituals, she found the benefits stayed with her throughout the day.

"Now I really notice it when I don't do my practices," she says.

Dimple's frame on healthy, nurturing daily habits as rituals shifted something for me. Her definition of a ritual is simply that it is a repetitive behaviour or habit that nurtures us or makes us happy. Most of us probably don't acknowledge these practices as rituals, and that's where we miss an opportunity. When we give a behaviour some intentionality – when we prioritize it and recognize it as having meaning and value – it becomes more powerful. And if you give a small practice a chance to make a difference, it becomes easier to add on and do more things that enhance your physical and mental well-being.

Dimple also pointed out that when life gets challenging, complicated, or unpredictable, it's valuable to have something that keeps you grounded and gives you strength. You may not see the benefit right away, but when challenges strike, you'll be in the best possible space to handle whatever comes at you.

I asked Dimple what her daily ritual looks like nowadays, given she's been at it for almost twenty years. She giggled.

"Many days, I devote two hours to my practices."

Two hours?

Sure, that's probably more time than you can spend. The basics are simple, though, and the amount of time flexes with whatever else is going on, even for someone like Dimple, who is an expert in self-care and rituals. She gets up early because she loves the sunrise. She drinks lemon water and green juice, takes some supplements, meditates for eleven – just eleven – minutes, writes in her journal, reads or listens to something inspiring, and will sometimes add on a spiritual or mystical practice like crystals or tarot. None of this is complicated, and I wager that you do at least some of these things. What you're probably missing is the sense of intention behind the practices, the commitment to a basic few as non-negotiable elements of your day, and a prioritization of yourself as worthy of that relatively small commitment.

REFLECTION

Finding – and creating – ease ironically takes effort and attention until the practices are so ingrained that it's more difficult to live without them. All of the women I know who live genuinely happy, purposeful, healthy lives are living role models of this practice and its possibilities. What these women have in common is that the determination that they are worth it and their ability to be who they want to be for the people they love and care for is directly proportional to the care they invest in themselves first.

I've come to realize that there's something dysfunctional in our society when it comes to how women tend to feel valuable. For some reason, we've collectively gotten into a habit of using our long to-do lists and martyred claiming to be "busy" or have "no time" as badges of honour. No one is going to change this but us.

11

THE WAY FORWARD

Now you have the RECEIVE framework. Let's recap.

R: Recognize your reality. Get clear on the immutable facts of where you are right now. No sugar coating, wishing, or sweeping under the rug. Just the facts.

E: Evaluate. What does it mean? Are you in an acceptable situation, or does something have to change? And will your answer be different in a month or a year?

C: Choose. Gather up your options, put together a list of the criteria you'll need to make the necessary decisions, and make them. No turning back. Start small if you have to, but move forward with courage and conviction.

E: Energy. You have limits, and you need to be clear about what gives you energy and what – and who – depletes you. Invest in yourself a little more to ensure you've got what you need for yourself and then for all of your other responsibilities. Take care of all of your energy operating systems.

I: Initiate. Figure out what you need and summon up the courage to go after it. Ask for it. Put yourself out there just a little bit with the intention of shoring up your support systems. After all, how many other people's support systems are you a part of?

V: Voice. Who are you, really? Have you forgotten someone that's hidden deep within you, behind all the responsibilities? Excavate, release, and explore. Do what you have to do in order to bring your unique voice back into the world.

E: Ease. Life rarely has to be as difficult as we choose to make it. But a life that includes more ease won't just happen; it's part practices and part the recognition of those practices as rituals that nourish any and all aspects of you.

Why do you persist in taking on too much, putting yourself last, ignoring the signs of a situation that's not working, and creating your life as a solo act?

What compels you to ignore or refuse offers of assistance and isolate yourself behind a wall of determined independence, while muting the intuitive voices that tell you what you need and want?

Why is it that you let something happen when you know it's going sideways?

Why don't you listen to that voice that's usually giving you great advice that, if you take it, will probably help you avoid a lot of drama and pain, not to mention time?

And what happens to you if you don't change?

Remember Glinda's message to Dorothy in *The Wizard of Oz*?

"You had the power all along."

Everything you need is already within you, including the power to choose what works for you and the strength to ask for help. You have more choices than you are seeing and more support than you're accessing, even if you haven't found or identified it yet.

When the deal was done on the perfect house, we had to undertake the process of disassembling the home we had lived in for the better part of twenty years, the home my boys had been living in since they were born, the home that housed a thousand memories and all of the stuff attached to those memories. To say I was overwhelmed would have been an understatement. Yet, true to form, I dove in and started the process, dumping things, throwing things in boxes, and generally creating a tornado of a mess.

One Saturday morning, just a few days before the moving truck was to arrive, a neighbour dropped by unannounced. I made an effort to be polite, wondering what she wanted.

"I've come to help you pack. I'm good at kitchens."

I'm sure my jaw dropped. And, of course, my first instinct was to decline politely but firmly. Did I want her to see how disorganized I was? Would she pack things the way I wanted them packed? A hundred objections flew through my mind in that instant.

"You need help. I'm here, and I'm offering. Are you going to let me in?"

She was smiling but firm. I stepped aside, and in she came. Several hours later, my kitchen was impeccably packed. It was the perfect gift, perfectly timed, and I had come close to turning it down.

Old habits die hard, and if we expect ourselves to be perfect, we will just get frustrated and continue the vicious cycle.

Work on progress, not perfection. And when someone offers, try saying yes.

12

CONCLUSION

Yes, you can do it all – just not at once, and not alone.

There are many women who have adopted some or most of the principles I've outlined here and found themselves better for it. Even a small shift towards receiving versus constantly giving is a step in the right direction. Whether a CEO or a small business owner, single or partnered, or parent or caregiver, almost every woman I know has more demands than available time and energy. Learning when to give and when to receive, when to be steadfast and when to change course, and when to retreat and when to swing on a pole or break into song are all lessons you can absorb a bit at a time. The women who have adopted some or all of the RECEIVE model have found themselves to be happier and better able to cope with whatever life sends their way.

I've shared some of my stories and experiences and given you a glimpse of what some other strong, smart women have struggled with in order to show you unequivocally that if you're both strong and struggling, you're not alone. In fact, you're completely normal.

I've invited you to consider that, if you learn better how to RECEIVE, you'll not only be happier yourself, but you'll be better able to do the things that are important to you in the world.

I hope that the end of this book is just the beginning of a journey for you – a journey that sees you better at allowing, accepting, inviting, and receiving with all of your inherent grace, strength, and pride intact – intact, but not in the way.

Let's understand strength as having grace and softness. Let's put away the Superwoman idea for once and for all and agree that we are better – stronger – together.

I believe that if more women can get more comfortable owning who they are, asking for what they need, and ensuring they're surrounding themselves with people they can count on, we are unstoppable. And with women thriving, the world is a better place.

Be the Intentional Alpha of your life.

ACKNOWLEDGMENTS

This book has been over a decade in the making, and anything that spans that long a period of time can't help but have had a multitude of influences. Following, please find my attempt to express my gratitude to as many as I can recall.

The clients – too many to count; every single one of whom has taught me something. I feel privileged to do the work I do, and I accept the trust that's placed in me with deep gratitude.

The Associates – the Parachute Executive Coaching coaches that make me look good every time they see a client. I respect your skill and professionalism, and I'm grateful for your patience as I attempt to grow the systems and processes that will take our little enterprise to its next level.

The communities – as an adult, it's typically hard to build new groups of friends, and I hit the jackpot twice in the past few years. The Good Life Project community under the leadership of Jonathan and Stephanie Fields and the Heroic Public Speaking community created by Michael and Amy Port have gifted me both with opportunities to grow personally and professionally and with legions of smart, world-changing friends and colleagues in every corner of the globe.

The masterminds – I've found myself in different small groups for different reasons in the past couple of years, and each has been a source of inspiration, support, and laughter. Thanks to Eliot, Scott, Kristina, Jane, Susan, D'Arcy, Trevor, Chris, and Damian for your time, your honest feedback, your unequivocal support, and your willingness to laugh at everything.

The women of Chief – the founders, the staff and the members who all inspire me, require me to bring my "A" game, and who are collectively creating a better world by putting more women into more positions of leadership and influence.

The princesses – a group of hilarious and brilliant women who inspired me to run the half marathon I thought I'd never do, who encouraged me through this writing process, and whose company every week for Zoom Cocktails through the 2020 lockdown has made the time pass just a little more easily.

Kristina Paider, writing coach extraordinaire and the author of *The Hollywood Approach,* has been a champion for this book ever since I mentioned the early germ of the idea. Being the trooper that she is, she spent a week with me on a beach in her Dominican Republic home, wrestling the ideas into some semblance of structure.

Angela Lauria, Madeline Kosten, and the rest of The Author Incubator team and community – if not for you, this book would have stayed in my head, probably forever.

And finally, the lads. The boys. No longer the teenagers. My sons, Brendan and Conor, you are the reason I do everything. I know some mothers are sad when their children strike out on their own, but your independence, resourcefulness, strength, and determination inspire me every day as I watch you make your ways in the world. I love you.

ABOUT THE AUTHOR

Karen Wright is one of the pioneers of the coaching profession and works with executives, founders, professionals, and entrepreneurs around the world to help them achieve the elusive combination of success, health, and happiness.

Karen's firm, Parachute Executive Coaching, was one of the first firms able to provide executive coaching on a global scale.

She is a Master Certified Coach, the top designation granted by the International Coaching Federation. Prior to becoming a professional coach, Karen worked in consumer-packaged goods marketing and advertising in Canada and the U.S.A. for both publicly-traded and privately-held companies.

Karen received her MBA from the Ivey School of Business and her BA in Economics from Western University. She completed coach training from two leading accredited schools and has taught for both schools. She is a Certified Health Coach from the Institute of Integrated Nutrition, has a certificate in applied positive psychology, has studied the neuroscience applications of coaching, and is a licensed mindfulness trainer.

Karen is a nationally-published columnist, a frequent contributor to various media, and a sought-after keynote speaker. Her first book, *The Complete Executive: The 10-Step System for Great Leadership Performance*, was released in September of 2012.

She lives in Toronto, Canada, when she's not in Paris or Costa Rica or adventuring elsewhere in the world.

ABOUT DIFFERENCE PRESS

DP

DIFFERENCE
PRESS

Difference Press is the exclusive publishing arm of The Author Incubator, an educational company for entrepreneurs – including life coaches, healers, consultants, and community leaders – looking for a comprehensive solution to get their books written, published, and promoted. Its founder, Dr. Angela Lauria, has been bringing to life the literary ventures of hundreds of authors-in-transformation since 1994.

A boutique-style self-publishing service for clients of The Author Incubator, Difference Press boasts a fair and easy-to-understand profit structure, low-priced author copies, and author-friendly contract terms. Most importantly, all of our #incubatedauthors maintain ownership of their copyright at all times.

LET'S START A MOVEMENT WITH YOUR MESSAGE

In a market where hundreds of thousands of books are published every year and are never heard from again, The Author Incubator is different. Not only do all Difference Press books reach Amazon bestseller status, but all of our authors are actively changing lives and making a difference.

Since launching in 2013, we've served over 500 authors who came to us with an idea for a book and were able to write it and get it self-published in less than 6 months. In addition, more than 100 of those books were picked up by traditional publishers and are now available in bookstores. We do this by selecting the highest quality and highest potential applicants for our future programs.

Our program doesn't only teach you how to write a book – our team of coaches, developmental editors, copy editors, art directors, and marketing experts incubate you from having a book idea to being a published, bestselling author, ensuring that the book you create can actually make a difference in the world. Then we give you the training you need to use your book to make the difference in the world, or to create a business out of serving your readers.

ARE YOU READY TO MAKE A DIFFERENCE?

You've seen other people make a difference with a book. Now it's your turn. If you are ready to stop watching and start taking massive action, go to http://theauthorincubator.com/apply/.

"Yes, I'm ready!"

OTHER BOOKS BY DIFFERENCE PRESS

Daddy Issues: The Guide to Heal Your Anger and Pain toward Your Father by Denise J. Anderson

Are We the Reason I'm Not Getting Pregnant?: The Fearlessly Fertile Method for Clearing the Blocks Between Your Relationship and Your Baby by Rosanne Austin

IMPACT Pharmacist: Start Your Own Wellness Practice and Leave Your Retail Pharmacy Job Behind! by Dr. Asha Bohannon and Eric Bohannon

I Want to Learn Energy Healing: The Guidebook for Teaching Others to Heal and Discovering the New Chakras Rays by Minh-Chau Craig

Clinician to Coach: Secrets to Building Your Successful Health Coach Empire by Dr. Jessica Drummond, DCN, CNS, PT, NBC-HWC

The Team Whisperer: Successfully Lead a Cross-Generation, Race, and Gender Team by Ell Graniel

Listen to Yourself: The Brown Girls' Guide to Trusting Your Intuition by Cindy A. Gunraj

*Holy Sh*t, I'm a Gifted "Misfit"!: The Young Folx Guide to Unlock Your Superpowers* by J.J. Kelly, PSY.D.

Unpacked: An Old Soul's Guide to the Art of Relocation by Christine Kraft

The Feminine Dating Revolution: The Zero-Heartache Way of Attracting the Love of Your Life by Rosine Kushnick

Help! I Need a Break from Motherhood: The Stay-at-Home Mom's Guide to a Balanced Life by K. Domiana Ndour

Break Free from Anxiety: A Practical Guide to Manage Your Anxiety and Love Your Life by Tonya M. Overton

Soul Places: The Star Child's Cosmic Atlas for Finding Heaven on Earth by Karinne Piat

FLOW: The Devotional for Grown Folks by Pam "The FLOW Boss" Reid

Inner Peace: Learn the Craft of Meditation and Use It as Medication by Catherine Scherwenka

The Art of Speaking in Front of the Camera: From Fear to Confidence on Video in the Digital Age by Lilia Sixtos

Make Rehab Clients Beg for Homework: The New Framework to Integrate Therapy into Daily Routines by Julie Smith

But I Want Both: The Working Mom's Guide to Creating a Life She Loves by Nina Sossamon-Pogue

The Beautiful Un-Becoming: The Ultimate Guide to Life after a Spiritual Awakening by Lyndsay K. R. Toensing

Free Yourself From Grief: The Secret to Moving on with Life After the Death of a Parent by Julie Tourangeau

Changing Birth on Earth: A Midwife and Nurse's Guide to Using Physiology to Avoid Another Unnecessary Cesarean by Gail Tully

The Financial Freedom Formula: Millionaire Secrets to Build Your Wealth by Jennifer Vavricka

Writing the High Vibe Hero's Journey: The Essential Structure to Crafting a Story that Changes the World by KristaLyn A. Vetovich

Betrayed: Recover from the Shock and Pain of Finding Out That Your Spouse Is Cheating by Dr. Jersey Wulster

Guerilla Startup: Unique Steps to Run and Sustain Your Business by Claudette Yarbrough

The Medicine Mage: 12 Steps from Depleted Doctor to Magic Healer of the New Earth by Xuemei Zhong

THANK YOU

Since you've finished reading this book, I know that you are on the path to redefining what it means for you to be both strong and open to receiving. I'd love to continue to support you on this journey.

Visit www.AccidentalAlpha.com for some free resources and for information about additional products, communities and programs.

And you can follow me on social media at any or all of the following:

Facebook: https://www.
Facebook.com/KarenWrightCoach
Instagram: @AccidentalAlphaWoman and @Karen-WrightCoach
Twitter: @KWrightCoach
LinkedIn: https://www.LinkedIn.com/in/Karen-WrightCoach